P9-AFE-817

GOLFER'S
GUIDE TO LIFE

GOLFER'S
GUIDE TO LIFE

*Wisdom & Wit Based
on the Realities of Golfing*

Copyright ©2004 Elm Hill Books, an imprint of J. Countryman®, a division of Thomas Nelson, Inc.
Nashville, TN 37214

All rights reserved. No part of this book may be reproduced, stored in a retrieval system, or transmitted in any form or by any means—electronic, mechanical, photocopying, recording, or any other—except for brief quotations in printed reviews, without prior written permission of the publisher.

The quoted ideas expressed in this book (but not scripture verses) are not, in all cases, exact quotations, as some have been edited for clarity and brevity. In all cases, the author has attempted to maintain the speaker's original intent. In some cases, quoted material for this book was obtained from secondary sources, primarily print media. While every effort was made to ensure the accuracy of these sources, the accuracy cannot be guaranteed. For additions, deletions, corrections or clarifications in future editions of this text, please write ELM HILL BOOKS.

For additions, deletions, corrections, or clarifications in future editions of this text, please contact Paul Shepherd, Executive Director for Elm Hill Books. Email pshepherd@elmhillbooks.com.

Scripture quotations are taken from:

New Century Version® (NCV) © 1987, 1988, 1991 by Thomas Nelson, Inc. All rights reserved. Used by permission.

The Holy Bible, New King James Version (NKJV) Copyright © 1982 by Thomas Nelson, Inc. Used by permission.

Cover Design by D/SR
Page Layout by Bart Dawson

ISBN 1-4041-8509-7

Printed in the United States of America

For Virginia Criswell

A Lifetime Supporter on and off the Links

TABLE OF CONTENTS

INTRODUCTION

Since that fateful day in 1963 when my dad came home with a paper bag containing four used clubs, I have been fascinated by golf. As a young boy, the game was simple: Swing away and hope. But as I matured, I began to appreciate the subtleties and beauty of the sport. Gradually, I came to the same realization that has touched the lives of countless duffers and pros alike: Golf is an awful lot like life.

Lee Trevino declared, "Golf is the most human game of all." Perhaps this helps explain the game's enduring popularity.

This book outlines ten principles which apply on or off the links. In support of these ideas, I have selected quotations (from great golfers *and* great thinkers) along with verses from the book of Proverbs. These principles, properly applied, may help lower your handicap—if so, that's good. But more importantly, these principles apply to the game that is played beyond the 18th green.

As you consider the words that follow, examine your own style of play. If you've been a believer in the "swing away and hope" method, it's time to reconsider. After all, whether it's the game of golf or the game of life, it's always a good time to improve your score.

Lesson 1:
LIFETIME LEARNING
Take a Lesson

Give instruction to a wise man, and he will be still wiser; Teach a just man, and he will increase in learning.

PROVERBS 9:9 NKJV

The stoic philosopher Epictetus observed, "No great thing is created suddenly." And so it is with a golf swing. Proper technique may take years to achieve and a lifetime to master. That's why the serious golfer understands that his education is ongoing.

Jack Nicklaus, perhaps the greatest golfer ever to swing a club, advised, "Don't be afraid to take a lesson. I'm not."

And if it's good enough for the Golden Bear, it's good enough for the rest of us.

ALWAYS KEEP LEARNING. IT KEEPS YOU YOUNG.

PATTY BERG

Learn from the skillful.
He who teaches himself,
hath a fool for his master.

BEN FRANKLIN

It takes twenty years to make
an overnight success.

EDDIE CANTOR

You must work very hard to become
a natural golfer.

GARY PLAYER

You build a good golf game like you
build a wall: one brick at a time.

TONY LEMA

It is easier to learn something new
than it is to unlearn something
that you have been doing wrong
for a long time.

HARVEY PENICK

Watch your golf swing on videotape.
In your mind, you may be Fred Couples.
On tape, you may be Fred Mertz.

GLEN WAGGONER

Nothing goes down slower than a golf handicap.

BOBBY NICHOLS

It does not matter how slowly you go
so long as you do not stop.

CONFUCIUS

He knows enough who knows
how to learn.

HENRY ADAMS

The average golfer is entirely capable
of building a repeating swing
and breaking 80.

BEN HOGAN

I think that, in golf, your physical and
mental capabilities aren't really
compatible until you're 35 to 45.
Those, to me, are your peak years.

RAYMOND FLOYD

I am still learning.

MICHELANGELO'S MOTTO

Golf is a microcosm of this world
in which we live—
a game rich in humanity.

C. GRANT SPAETH

Nothing is impossible to a willing heart.

JOHN HEYWOOD

There is nothing in this game of golf
that can't be improved upon—
if you practice.

PATTY BERG

Work to become, not acquire.

ELBERT HUBBARD

Golf is perpetual loss and rediscovery.

THOMAS BOSWELL

I PROBABLY HAVE FORGOTTEN MORE ABOUT GOLF THAN I WILL EVER LEARN. WHAT YOU DO IS REMEMBER SOME OF THE THINGS YOU THOUGHT YOU'D NEVER FORGET.

⬤ JACK NICKLAUS ⬤

The secret of golf is to get
a complex mortal to simplify positions
and actions as much as possible.

TOMMY ARMOUR

The game is most fun when you
are experimenting.

JACK NICKLAUS

Mistakes are their own instructors.

HORACE

Every cure is temporary.
But it's nice while it lasts.

JACK NICKLAUS

The doer alone learneth.

NIETZSCHE

If you're smart, you learn something from
every round you play.

SAM SNEAD

It takes just as long to play
your way out of a slump as it does
to play your way into one.

HARVEY PENICK

Don't consider losses a waste of time.
Consider them an apprenticeship.

GREG NORMAN

Improvement lies in narrowing the margin
between your best and worst shots.

JACK NICKLAUS

Many amateurs have a tendency to
overdo instruction. It's like the old saying,
"A couple of aspirin might cure
what ails you, but the whole bottle
will probably kill you."

SAM SNEAD

All human power is a compound
of time and patience.

HONORÉ DE BALZAC

What we have to learn to do,
we learn by doing.

ARISTOTLE

It is part of the cure to wish to be cured.

SENECA

I learned to play golf from Nelson
and Hogan, which is like learning to paint from
Michelangelo and Leonardo.

KEN VENTURI

When the pupil is ready,
the teacher will come.

CHINESE SAYING

Knowledge is power.

FRANCIS BACON

No man ever became wise by chance.

SENECA

Preparation through steady practice
is the only honest avenue to achieving
your potential.

CHI CHI RODRIGUEZ

Every day you miss playing or practicing
is one day longer it takes to be good.

BEN HOGAN

Remember what you are taught, and
listen carefully to words of knowledge.

PROVERBS 23:12 NCV

LESSON 2:
COURAGE

Go for the Green

---

*Keep your eyes focused on what is right,
and look straight ahead to what is good.*
PROVERBS 4:25 NCV

Whether we're on the links or off, each of us must find a balance between foolish bravado and needless fear. We must decide whether to follow our dreams or to recoil from our worst nightmares. Our choices, taken as a whole, make us who we are. And while there are no hard and fast guidelines, history seems to show that, on balance, courage is its own reward.

Two thousand years ago, Tacitus observed, "The desire for safety stands against every great and noble enterprise." spoken like a man standing in the fairway of a par five who is about to go for the green in two.

Golf is the "only-est" sport. You're completely alone with every conceivable opportunity to defeat yourself.

● Hale Irwin ●

The fearful Unbelief is unbelief in yourself.

THOMAS CARLYLE

Great players know how—and when—
to be aggressive.

GREG NORMAN

I feel more comfortable attacking
the course rather than playing it cautiously.

ARNOLD PALMER

All fear is a sign of want of faith.

MOHANDAS GANDHI

Golf may not teach character,
but it reveals it.

THOMAS BOSWELL

Golf tells you much about character.
Play a round of golf with someone, and you
know them more intimately than you might
from years of dinner parties.

HARVEY PENICK

Success in golf depends less on strength
of body than upon strength of mind
and character.

ARNOLD PALMER

I never pray that I may win.
I just ask for the courage to do my best.

GARY PLAYER

CHARACTER IS DESTINY.

● HERACLITUS ●

Remember golf presents no physical danger.

● Bobby Jones ●

The best players fail the most because
they are in the hunt all the time.

DEANE BEMAN

I think players have a fear of finding out
their true limits, which is even greater than
their fear of failure.

PETER JACOBSEN

Ask yourself, "What's the worst
that can happen?" Prepare to accept it.
Then improve upon the worst.

DALE CARNEGIE

No matter what happens,
I can always dig ditches.

ARNOLD PALMER

Some say, "Be patient." Then I hear,
"Just let it happen." Then there are guys who
"make it happen."

TOM KITE

The two things that motivate me most
are fear of failure and
a desire for self-improvement.

JACK NICKLAUS

Trust your hopes, not your fears.

DAVID MAHONEY

Most golfers prepare for disaster.
A good golfer prepares for success.

BOB TOSKI

I'm not about to quit. You just gotta keep
beating the ball, grit your teeth
and make birdies.

JIM THORPE

Your reach and your grasp should be
the same. That's the way to be happy.
Reach for the furthest thing you think
you can get. Then reach again. Sooner or later,
the things that looked way beyond you
are the next natural goal to reach.

CALVIN PEETE

He conquers who endures.

PERSIUS

Keep hitting it straight until the wee ball
goes in the hole.

JAMES BRAID

The first and great commandment is
don't let them scare you.

ELMER DAVIS

Courage is the price life extracts
for granting peace.

AMELIA EARHART

A buoyant, positive approach to
the game is as basic as a sound swing.

TONY LEMA

When in doubt, do the courageous thing.

JAN SMUTS

BE DECISIVE. A WRONG DECISION IS GENERALLY LESS DISASTROUS THAN INDECISION.

● BERNHARD LANGER ●

HAPPINESS IS A FORM OF COURAGE.

● HOLBROOK JACKSON ●

FAITH IS IN
YOUR HEART.
CONFIDENCE IS IN
YOUR MIND
AS WELL AS
YOUR HEART.
IN GOLF, TRUE
CONFIDENCE WILL
ALWAYS BEAT
BLIND FAITH.

● HARVEY PENICK ●

I like the feeling of trying my hardest
under pressure.

TIGER WOODS

To win, you must treat a pressure
situation as an opportunity to succeed,
not an opportunity to fail.

GARDNER DICKINSON

The greatest single lesson to be learned
from golf is mental discipline.

LOUISE SUGGS

The wise see danger ahead and avoid it, but
fools keep going and get into trouble.

PROVERBS 22:3 NCV

LESSON 3:
ATTITUDE

Believe in Your Swing

---

*Understanding is like a fountain
which gives life to those who use it.*
PROVERBS 16:22 NCV

Marcus Aurelius observed, "Man must be arched and buttressed from within, else the temple waivers to the dust." And like a good man or woman, a good golf game depends almost entirely upon inner strength.

Gary Player wrote, "There's absolutely no question that golf is a game of mind over matter." In this chapter, we consider ways to improve one's golf score by improving one's attitude.

All too often, a bogey is simply a physical manifestation of the self-fulfilling prophesy. We become better golfers once we convince ourselves that the same may be said of birdies.

I THINK THAT TO SCORE IN GOLF IS A MATTER OF CONFIDENCE.

● HENRY COTTON ●

You have more potential than you think.

SAM SNEAD

In my opinion, the average golfer
underestimates himself.

BEN HOGAN

Self-confidence is the first requisite
to great undertakings.

SAMUEL JOHNSON

They can because they think they can.

VIRGIL

Try to think where you want to put
the ball, not where you don't
want it to go.

BILLY CASPER

YOU ARE WHAT YOU THINK YOU ARE, IN GOLF AND IN LIFE.

◉ RAYMOND FLOYD ◉

I'M AS GOOD A PLAYER AS I THINK I AM. IF YOU CAN'T WIN IN YOUR OWN DREAMS, FORGET IT.

● CALVIN PEETE ●

The hardest thing is to *believe*
that *you* can get to the top.

JIM THORPE

Man is what he believes.

ANTON CHEKHOV

A bad attitude is worse than a bad swing.

PAYNE STEWART

I don't dwell on bad shots, bad rounds,
or bad tournaments. I don't play in the past.
I play in the present.

RAYMOND FLOYD

Clear your mind of can't.

SAMUEL JOHNSON

DON'T GIVE UP ON PROPER THINKING JUST BECAUSE IT DOESN'T WORK ONE DAY.

TOM WATSON

THE PERFECT ROUND OF GOLF HAS NEVER BEEN PLAYED. IT'S 18 HOLES-IN-ONE. I ALMOST DREAMT IT ONCE, BUT I LIPPED OUT AT 18.

◉ BEN HOGAN ◉

When I'm on, golf has no strategy.
I drill every shot at the pin. I want to hole out
from the fairway.

LANNY WADKINS

When I'm in a zone, I don't think about
the shot or the wind or the distance or
the gallery or anything;
I just pull a club and swing.

MARK CALCAVECCHIA

When I play my best golf, I feel as if
I'm in a fog, standing back watching
the earth in orbit with a golf club
in my hands.

MICKEY WRIGHT

You have to train the mind for success.

◉ Calvin Peete ◉

THE BEST WAY TO BUILD CONFIDENCE IS TO SUCCEED.

● LEE TREVINO ●

Few athletes trust their minds as much
as their muscles.

THOMAS BOSWELL

When the great player makes a mistake,
he says, "I'm going to work on that and
not do it again." The bad player says,
"Boy, I messed up again.
I guess I really am a dog."

PETER JACOBSEN

Human thoughts have the tendency to
turn themselves into
their physical equivalents.

EARL NIGHTINGALE

Assume a virtue if you have it not.

WILLIAM SHAKESPEARE

The pessimist complains about the wind;
the optimist expects it to change;
the realist adjusts the sails.

WILLIAM ARTHUR WARD

My father told me, "You must never
learn to think the negative."

JOHNNY MILLER

Whether you think you can
or think you can't, you're right.

HENRY FORD

Don't look for excuses to loose.
Look for excuses to win.

CHI CHI RODRIGUEZ

DON'T LINGER TOO LONG IN THINKING ABOUT YOUR SHOTS— GOOD OR BAD— BUT STAMP THE GOOD ONES INTO YOUR MIND FOR FUTURE REFERENCE.

● GREG NORMAN ●

THE MOST IMPORTANT THING FOR ME IN PREPARING FOR MAJOR TOURNAMENTS IS BASIC PEACE OF MIND.

● JACK NICKLAUS ●

IF A PLAYER IS CONFIDENT IN THE CLUB HE HAS SELECTED, THAT CONFIDENCE IS REFLECTED IN HIS SWING.

● CARY MIDDLECOFF ●

The brain controls the mind.
The mind controls the body.
The body controls the club.

MIKE HEBRON

Make up your mind before your
backswing starts, then let your muscles
do the work.

TOMMY ARMOUR

The more time I have to think about
a shot, the worse I'm going to hit it.

LARRY LAORETTI

The man who insists upon seeing
with perfect clearness before he decides,
never decides.

HENRI FRÉDÉRIC AMIEL

Be yourself. Play your own game.
HARVEY PENICK

Simplicity is the answer. I only check
three things—my timing, my balance and
my square hand position at address.
CALVIN PEETE

Go from strength to strength.
GREG NORMAN

Golf is more a game of head and heart
than of guts and muscle.
THOMAS BOSWELL

Never think about what you did wrong on the last shot. Think about what you will do right on the next one.

TOMMY ARMOUR

There is nothing final about a mistake, except its being taken as final.

PHYLISS BOTTOME

Our greatest foes, and whom we chiefly combat, are within.

MIGUEL DE CERVANTES

Prayer has given me the strength, concentration and confidence necessary to perform a seemingly impossible task.

DICK CHAPMAN,
WINNER OF THE 1949 CANADIAN AMATEUR

Golf makes one loathe mediocrity.

GARY PLAYER

The fellow who wins is the fellow
who thinks he can win.

GAY BREWER

The happiness of your life depends
upon the quality of your thoughts;
therefore, guard accordingly.

MARCUS AURELIUS

Very often, what a man feels he is doing is more important than what he does.

● BOBBY JONES ●

Golf is 20 percent mechanics and technique.
The other 80 percent is philosophy, humor,
tragedy, romance, melodrama, companionship,
camaraderie, cussedness and conversation.

GRANTLAND RICE

Do your best, one shot at a time
and then move on.
Remember that golf is just a game.

NANCY LOPEZ

A merry heart does good, like medicine.

PROVERBS 17:22 NKJV

LESSON 4:
CONCENTRATION
Keep Your Head Down

Enthusiasm without knowledge is not good.
If you act too quickly, you might make a mistake.
PROVERBS 19:2 NCV

Since the better part of golf is played between the ears, it's no accident that the game's most popular adage concerns the human head. All golfers, from time to time, fall prey to the powerful temptation to look up before the swing is completed. The results are predictable: Curiosity kills the cat, or, in this case, the birdie.

In golf, as in life, concentration is rewarded at every turn. When we attend to the job at hand, the game seems to flow. But as distractions increase, so do bogeys.

If you're looking for a surefire way to lower your handicap, learn the fine art of concentration. If you keep your head down during the swing, you can hold your head high after the swing is over.

On the golf course, concentrate on the present, forget the past, and don't look too far ahead.

● JUDY RANKIN ●

Maintaining your composure on the golf course is worth at least three shots a round.

● Billy Casper ●

Some golfers I've met can't achieve total
concentration because they're too brilliant for
their own good. They over-analyze.

SAM SNEAD

When you're afraid, keep your mind on
what you have to do. And if you have
been thoroughly prepared,
you will not be afraid.

DALE CARNEGIE

Focus not on the commotion around you
but on the opportunity ahead of you.

ARNOLD PALMER

Become so wrapped up in something
that you forget to be afraid.

LADY BIRD JOHNSON

In golf, the hands are the chief point
of concentration.

HARRY VARDON

This game is like a horse. If you take
your eye off it, it'll jump back and
kick your shins.

BYRON NELSON

At its best, the U. S. Open demands
the patience of St. Francis and
the will of General George Patton.

THOMAS BOSWELL

To be disciplined from within, where all
is permissible, where all is concealed—
that is the point.

MICHEL DE MONTAIGNE

Golf is you against yourself.

JACK NICKLAUS

All serious doubts start from within.

EUDORA WELTY

Teach yourself to work in uncertainty.

BERNARD MALAMUD

What you think while you're playing golf
is probably the most important
single part of your game.

GARY PLAYER

The mind messes up more shots than the body.

TOMMY BOLT

Many golfers can't concentrate because
they're too self-conscious.

SAM SNEAD

Always put score ahead of pride.

KEN VENTURI

The scoring at golf is as much about
avoiding disasters as making birdies.

JACK NICKLAUS

Golf is a game of mistakes.
The best players make the smallest mistakes.

SAM SNEAD

PATIENCE IS BETTER THAN STRENGTH.

● PROVERBS 16:32 NCV ●

LESSON 5:
PREPARATION
Groove Your Swing

Listen carefully to wisdom;
set your mind on understanding.

PROVERBS 2:2 NCV

The philosopher Epictetus advised his students, "Practice, for heaven's sake, in the little things; and then proceed to greater." Although Epictetus was certainly no golfer, his advice still applies on the links. A sound golf swing is never built overnight. But with consistent effort, small strides on the practice tee produce big results on the score card.

A twenty-nine-year-old accountant named Julius Boros decided to take a chance on the PGA tour. Because he had taken time to build a solid swing, Boros quickly earned a reputation for consistency. Eventually, he won two U. S. Opens and a place in the Hall of Fame.

Boros advised, "Think of your golf swing as a machine. Build the most efficient machine you can." If *you* want to build an efficient striking machine, carefully consider each facet of the golf swing. Then groove those fundamentals into your swing. Whether you're an accountant or a philosopher, great things are sure to follow.

My only goal is to improve my golf swing.
Everything else will take care of itself.

TOM WATSON

I grew up knowing you cannot be
a success in life if you don't work hard.

GARY PLAYER

The amount you are willing to work
on your game will determine how much
of your potential you will realize.

KEN VENTURI

God gives talent.
Work transforms talent into genius.

ANNA PAVLOVA

I ADVOCATE
WORKING HARD ON
THE FUNDAMENTALS
AND THEN WORKING
THE FUNDAMENTALS
INTO YOUR GAME.

● BEN HOGAN ●

Never lose the will to improve.

TOM WATSON

Goals are the fuel of progress.

GREG NORMAN

Setting goals is an art. The trick is setting
them at the right level—
neither too highnor too low.

GREG NORMAN

When a man's willing and eager,
the gods join in.

AESCHYLUS

Practice your swing until it becomes a habit of mind and muscle.

◉ Sam Snead ◉

To learn new habits is everything,
for it is to reach the substance of life.
Life is but a tissue of habits.

HENRI FRÉDÉRIC AMIEL

My goal? Consistency.
I try to do the same thing each time out.

GREG NORMAN

The simple swing that is also sound
will be susceptible to repetition.

BOBBY JONES

Don't be too anxious to see good results
on the scoreboard until you've fully
absorbed the principles of the golf swing
on the practice tee.

LOUISE SUGGS

Even a flawed swing can be effective
if it is repeatable.

CARY MIDDLECOFF

All the vital technical parts of the swing take
place in back of you, or above the head.
It's terrifying to think of all the gremlins
that can creep into your game.
The margin for error is infinitesimal.

ROGER MALTBIE

Once you've grooved your swing,
you shouldn't be conscious of making
any fundamental changes,
no matter what club you are using.

BEN HOGAN

The best swing is the one that repeats.

LEE TREVINO

The purpose of the waggle is to avoid
and destroy tension.

BOBBY JONES

Feel the club.

JIM FLICK

The waggle gives you the feeling of
the club in your hands.

JULIUS BOROS

There is no one, standard, correct grip size
for everyone. It all comes down to feel.

KEN VENTURI

Good golf begins with a good grip.

BEN HOGAN

Unless you have a reasonably good grip and
stance, anything you read about
the golf swing is useless.

HARVEY PENICK

A backswing that is too short inevitably goes
with a grip that is too tight.

BOBBY JONES

The cardinal principle in all golf shot-making
is that if you move your head,
you ruin your body action.

TOMMY ARMOUR

The key to a good swing is maintaining balance.

GARY MCCORD

In golf, there is never a single reason for success.

SAM SNEAD

MY GOAL IS TO HIT THE PERFECT SHOT EVERY TIME I SWING AT IT.

● TOM WATSON ●

LET YOUR GOALS BE IMPORTANT ENOUGH TO OVERRIDE YOUR DISTRACTIONS.

● BILLY CASPER ●

I want to make this game easy.
Improving my swing is a simplifying principle.
It eliminates a lot of clutter, a lot of false issues.

TOM WATSON

A simple tip to improve timing is this:
Pause briefly at the top of the backswing.

TOMMY ARMOUR

Nobody ever swung a golf club too slowly.

BOBBY JONES

The most common practice error is to
drift aimlessly to the range and start banging
balls at random. This isn't practice.
This is a waste of time. The worst thing
you can do is to practice your mistakes.

TONY LEMA

Unless by pure accident, no good ever comes from a bad stroke.

◉ Harry Vardon ◉

You'll never learn to learn to play golf on a golf course.

● Lee Trevino ●

To get the most from practice,
you have to have a plan.

SAM SNEAD

The good player doesn't experiment
or force changes during a round.

KEN VENTURI

Practice barefoot sometimes.
It'll give you a better sense of feel and
slow down your swing.

SAM SNEAD

What a shame to waste great shots
on the practice tee.

WALTER HAGEN

THERE'S MUCH MORE TO LEARNING HOW TO HIT GOOD GOLF SHOTS THAN BELTING OUT A FEW MILLION BALLS.

⬤ JACK NICKLAUS ⬤

First deserve, then desire.

@ English Proverb @

The way to build your swing is through
intelligent practice.

CARY MIDDLECOFF

Playing tournament golf without
practice is like walking downstairs
in pitch darkness.

THOMAS BOSWELL

A faulty swing ties you up so that
a smooth stroke becomes impossible.

BOBBY JONES

There is only one swing: the correct one.

ERNEST JONES

A lot of players have the talent but not
the drive to win. There are also guys who want
to be the best and who really work at it, but
who don't have the talent.

JACK NICKLAUS

People tell me, "You got it made."
I know better. I know where I came from.
I've got to work three times as
hard to stay where I am.

JIM THORPE

This game is about as close to
the American Dream as you can get.
The harder you work, the more respect you get.

JOHN MAHAFFEY

Luck is the residue of design.

BRANCH RICKEY

You can't go into a golf shop and
buy a good game.

SAM SNEAD

The world took six days.
Your golf swing may take a little longer.

GLEN WAGGONER

He who labors diligently need never despair;
for all things are accomplished
by diligence and labor.

MENANDER

For a righteous man may fall seven times
and rise again.

PROVERBS 24:16 NKJV

LESSON 6:
SELF-CONTROL
As Your Temper Rises, So Does Your Score

Patient people have great understanding, but people with quick tempers show their foolishness.
PROVERBS 14:29 NCV

During his heyday, Tommy Bolt's temper was infamous. Bolt could fling a club with the best of them. In fact, Jimmy Demaret proclaimed, "Tommy Bolt's putter had more air time than Lindbergh." But even the mercurial Bolt knew the value of self-control. He once admitted, "It's a game of patience." So much for air-born putters.

Publilius Syrus once observed, "Anger tortures itself." It might be added that on golf courses—or off—runaway emotions are the most dangerous hazards.

Golf is A NON-VIOLENT GAME PLAYED VIOLENTLY FROM WITHIN.

⚫ Bob Toski ⚫

More than any other game, golf is about
self-control, restraint of personality,
and the mastering of the emotions.

THOMAS BOSWELL

Over-aggression has never won
a golf tournament.

JACK NICKLAUS

Have patience with all things,
but first of all with yourself.

ST. FRANCIS OF SALES

Golf may be a sophisticated game. At least,
it is usually played with the outward appearance
of great dignity. It is, nevertheless,
a game of considerable passion, either
of the explosive type, or that which burns
inwardly and sears the soul.

BOBBY JONES

Patience is power.

CHINESE PROVERB

The most exquisitely satisfying act in the world
of golf is that of throwing a club.
The full backswing, the delayed wrist
action, the flowing follow-through,
followed by that unique whirring sound,
reminiscent only of a flock of passing
starlings, is without parallel in sport.

HENRY LONGHURST

It is the poor craftsman who blames his tools.

GLEN WAGGONER

Trouble once begun may never come
to an end until the card is torn
into a thousand fragments.

BERNARD DARWIN

Golf is the humbling game and
none know that better than the best.

THOMAS BOSWELL

A LOT OF TIMES YOU DON'T ACTUALLY WIN SO MUCH AS THE OTHER GUYS LOSE.

JACK NICKLAUS

Staying in the present is the key to any golfer's
game. Once you start thinking about a shot you
just messed up or what you have to do on
the next nine to catch somebody, you're lost.

PAUL AZINGER

No man can succeed at golf until he has
mastered the art of not permitting one bad hole,
or indeed one bad shot, to affect
the rest of his game.

HENRY LONGHURST

The hardest thing in golf is controlling
your emotions. You're facing a dead-still object,
something you can only address with your club
after a long wait. Your hands are tied in knots
and your mind begins to wander.
You must find a release from the tension.

JOANNE CARNER

IF YOU LET THE LAST SHOT INTERFERE WITH THE NEXT ONE, YOU CHEAT YOURSELF.

● CURTIS STRANGE ●

WHEN PEOPLE HEAR
THE WORD CONTROL
IN REGARD TO GOLF, THEY
USUALLY THINK IT MEANS
BEING CONSERVATIVE.
I DISAGREE. BEING IN
CONTROL MEANS MAKING
INTELLIGENT DECISIONS—
KNOWING WHEN TO BE
AGGRESSIVE AND WHEN
TO BE CAUTIOUS.

● CURTIS STRANGE ●

THINK LIKE A MAN OF ACTION, ACT LIKE A MAN OF THOUGHT.

◉ HENRI BERGSON ◉

To mourn a mischief that is past and gone Is the next way to draw new mischief on.

● WILLIAM SHAKESPEARE ●

Do not weep; do not wax indignant.
Understand.

BARUCH SPINOZA

Never let emotions interfere with
the ability to make smart decisions.

CURTIS STRANGE

Remember the game is played one stroke
at a time. You can't play the next shot
until you've played this one.

MARY LENA FAULK

Society has made us so aware of wanting
instant results that people have forgotten
the fundamentals that have to be
under control before they can succeed,
whether it's in business, golf or life.

JIM FLICK

True aggressiveness is based not on self-idolatry
or self-pity; it is based on self-knowledge.

GREG NORMAN

Play within yourself—play your own game.

BILLY CASPER

You can always find a distraction
if you're looking for one.

TOM KITE

He is next to the gods whom reason impels.

CLAUDIUS

Give it your best, but if somebody beats you fair
and square, congratulate him and move on.

GREG NORMAN

The only bruises in golf are to the spirit.

THOMAS BOSWELL

There are two things the players on tour
should realize:
Adults will copy your swing, and
young people will follow your example.

HARVEY PENICK

Misfortunes one can endur— they come
from outside, they are accidents.
But to suffer for one's own fault—ah—
there is the sting of life.

OSCAR WILDE

Golf, it has now long since been forgotten,
is essentially a simple pastime wherein you start
at A and hole out at B, overcoming as best you
may such hazards as you encounter on the way.

HENRY LONGHURST

You tend to get impatient with less-than-perfect
shots, but you have to remember that
less-than-perfect shots win Opens.

CURTIS STRANGE

Wise men turn away wrath.

PROVERBS 29:8 NKJV

LESSON 7:
RELAXATION

Swing Easy, Hit Hard

Worry is a heavy load.
PROVERBS 12:25 NCV

In golf, power is paradoxical. Overswinging destroys both balance and tempo, resulting in decreased accuracy and distance. In the tee box, the law of unintended consequences is alive and well: When we swing too hard, our shots fall short.

Recalling his days on the tour, Byron Nelson noted, "We thought that strength denied touch and that you could not consistently hit the ball long and straight. It's been proved that you can."

The same principles that provide power on the golf course also make us more effective in other areas of our lives. Life, like that little dimpled golf ball, can't be overpowered. So the best course of action, no matter where we find ourselves, is to swing easy and hit hard.

Overswinging does not produce power.
JUDY RANKIN

No good player ever swings as hard as he can.
ARNOLD PALMER

The length of a drive depends
not upon brute force,
but upon the speed of the clubhead.
BOBBY JONES

To hit the ball farther, don't swing faster
or harder. Make a fuller, more fluid swing.
That's how you get more clubhead speed.
BETH DANIEL

DON'T PRESS.
YOU CAN HIT HARD
WITHOUT PRESSING.

● HARRY VARDON ●

Golf is a game based not only on an intellectual
understanding but also on sensitivity for
the instrument. You can't bully your way
to a good golf swing.

JIM FLICK

Tension is golf's worst enemy.

BOBBY JONES

Too many people try to overpower
the golf ball like they do their businesses.

JIM FLICK

Golf is a walk in the park,
not a 400-meter dash.

TOM WATSON

A controlled shot to a closely guarded
green is the surest test of any man's golf.

A. W. TILLINGHAST

The busier you keep yourself with
the details of a particular shot,
the less time your mind has to dwell on the
emotional "ifs" and "buts."

JACK NICKLAUS

Fear ruins more golf shots
than any other factor.

TOMMY ARMOUR

We hope vaguely but dread precisely.

PAUL VALÉRY

The challenge in a golf stroke is to maintain
a perfect balance between firmness
and relaxation in the interests of control
and rhythm.

BOBBY JONES

Your ideal tempo is the maximum speed
at which you can control your body
and the club.

AL GEIBERGER

I've always tried to swing at about 85 percent
of my top speed. That's a pace I can control.

SAM SNEAD

Every good golfer possesses a carefully
developed set of key swing thoughts that
he uses to keep his game in balance.

JACK NICKLAUS

Standing over the shot, put everything out of
your mind except one key technical thought
and a "feel" for timing.

SAM SNEAD

The best cure for the body is to quiet the mind.

NAPOLEON I

Mental discipline, muscle memory.
Practice until you don't have to think.
CALVIN PEETE

The chains of habit are too weak to
be felt until they are too strong
to be broken.
SAMUEL JOHNSON

You have to find a way to rise above—
or drop below—anxiety. You have to find
a trance, some kind of self-hypnosis
that's almost a state of grace.
HALE IRWIN

I don't go into a trance when I address
the ball, but I come close.
SAM SNEAD

Confidence comes from hitting enough
good shots that you know you can do it again.
Whistling in the dark
is not the answer.

HARVEY PENICK

Education is hanging on
until you've caught on.

ROBERT FROST

Luck is not chance, it's Toil.
Fortune's expensive smile is earned.

EMILY DICKINSON

Start your downswing in a leisurely
fashion, in no hurry coming down,
with the acceleration smooth and natural.

BOBBY JONES

Lift the club with a light grip, so that it feels
heavy, like using an ax. You don't hit with
an ax, you accelerate it. That is exactly what
you should do with a golf club.

PETER THOMSON

Hum your favorite waltz and swing
to the beat of the tune.

SAM SNEAD

Tension is the product of technique or
temperament, or both, and
it just eats up the golf swing.

SAM SNEAD

Hit against a firm left side, but hit with
the right side. That's the source of power.

CALVIN PEETE

When it comes time to hit, don't leap at
the ball, but keep on swinging until
the ball has had a good start down
the fairway, and the clubhead
has done its job.

BOBBY JONES

Swing with ease against a breeze.

GOLF DIGEST TIP

WHY ARE OUR PRACTICE SWINGS THE BEST SWINGS? WE DON'T THINK ABOUT THE BALL, ONLY THE FLOW.

◉ KEN VENTURI ◉

For a good golf score, anxiety is fatal.

CARY MIDDLECOFF

Most golfers are not thinking,
even when they believe they are.
They are only worrying.

HARVEY PENICK

It's time to stop thinking, stop talking,
and start playing.

JACK NICKLAUS

Blessed are those who forget, for they
thus surmount even their own mistakes.

NIETZSCHE

When I swing, my mind is blank,
and my body is as loose as a goose.

SAM SNEAD

GOOD SENSE WILL PROTECT YOU; UNDERSTANDING WILL GUARD YOU.

● PROVERBS 2:11 NCV ●

LESSON 8:
MATURITY
Make Every Shot Count

The plans of hard-working people earn a profit,
but those who act too quickly become poor.
PROVERBS 21:5 NCV

Eight centuries before the birth of Christ, the Greek poet Hesiod advised, "It is best to do things systematically since we are only human, and disorder is our worst enemy." His advice applies to life and links.

More recently, Jack Nicklaus asked, "How many shots would you have saved if you never lost your temper, never got down on yourself, always developed strategy before hitting, and always played within your capabilities?" Most of us are too embarrassed to answer.

The game of golf rewards maturity. So does the game of life. Plan accordingly.

On every hole, never tee it up without a plan.
JULIUS BOROS

Good people order and arrange.
CONFUCIUS

Action before thought is the ruination
of most of your shots.
TOMMY ARMOUR

Imagine first that the present is past and,
second, that the past may yet be changed
and amended.
VIKTOR FRANKL

You must be thoughtful if you want
to get ahead in golf.

HARRY VARDON

After you've grooved your swing,
you still have to master the tactics of
getting around the course.
A good swing is small satisfaction
if you can't break 100.

SAM SNEAD

I never hit a shot, even in practice,
without having a very sharp
in-focus picture of it in my head.

JACK NICKLAUS

Always visualize your shot.

KEN VENTURI

DON'T JUST PLAY YOUR WAY AROUND THE COURSE. *THINK* YOUR WAY AROUND THE COURSE.

⚇ SAM SNEAD ⚇

The key to golf is to play the ball to
the best position from which
to play the next shot.

ARNOLD PALMER

Course management is like being in
a chess game. You're maneuvering
for position.

PATTY SHEEHAN

Play the shot you've got the greatest
chance of playing well.

TOMMY ARMOUR

A golf course is never quite the same from
one day to the next. So you have to be able to
meet the course on *its* terms, not your own.

BILLY CASPER

Preparing yourself for the course
you're about to play is a big part
of course management.

BILLY CASPER

Forewarned, forearmed; to be prepared
is half the victory.

MIGUEL DE CERVANTES

The essence of knowledge is, having it,
to use it.

CONFUCIUS

Great players learn that they don't need
to play their best golf to win. They only need to
shoot the lowest score.

TOM WATSON

The best strategic advice is this:
Know your strengths and take advantage of
them.

GREG NORMAN

Don't be afraid to be patient.

CURTIS STRANGE

Something really clicked on the day
I finally discovered the meaning of playing
within myself. Ever since, the game
has seemed a lot easier.

TIGER WOODS

Every golfer scores better when
he learns his capabilities.

TOMMY ARMOUR

Don't be ashamed to play safe.

ARNOLD PALMER

There's no rule in golf that states
"thou shall shoot for the flagstick."

PATTY SHEEHAN

The champion is the fellow who
can make the fewest poor shots.

TOMMY ARMOUR

The only thing that can get in the way
of a golfer's success is the golfer himself.

BILLY CASPER

One of the worst mistakes you can make
in golf is trying to *force* the game.

JACK NICKLAUS

THE BEST ADVICE I CAN GIVE ANY GOLFER ABOUT PLAYING FAIRWAY SHOTS IS: DON'T BE GREEDY.

◉ GARY PLAYER ◉

Every hole is a little tournament of its own.

TOM WATSON

The strategy of a golf course is the soul
of the game.

GEORGE THOMAS, JR.

The final round of the U. S. Open is not
so much a test of golf as a test of judgment.

JACK NICKLAUS

Golf is like chess. You have to think
ahead. Plot the hole back from the flag.

TOM WATSON

I have seen many really good players
attempt shots they should have known
were impossible.

BOBBY JONES

To attempt the impossible is always
a fault; to do so repeatedly is fatal.

MACHIAVELLI

You don't have to hit the ball perfectly
to win; you have to manage yourself better.

TOM WATSON

True valor lies in the middle,
between cowardice and rashness.

MIGUEL DE CERVANTES

Reckless gambles add needless strokes.

BOB GOALBY

Too much ambition is a bad thing to have
in a bunker.

BOBBY JONES

Never let one bad shot disrupt your rhythm or
concentration.

SAM SNEAD

There's a little boy in all of us. The trick
is knowing how to let that child come out.

MAC O'GRADY

Most matches are lost through
carelessness at the beginning
than any other cause.

HARRY VARDON

Every shot counts. The three-foot putt
is just as important as the 300-yard drive.

HENRY COTTON

MISSING A SHORT PUTT DOESN'T MEAN THAT I HAVE TO HIT MY NEXT DRIVE OUT-OF-BOUNDS.

● TONY LEMA ●

It takes knowledge to fill a home with rare and beautiful treasures.

⦿ Proverbs 24:4 ncv ⦿

LESSON 9:

ACCEPTANCE

Play It Where It Lies

Respect for the Lord will teach you wisdom.
If you want to be honored, you must be humble.
PROVERBS 15:33 NCV

After a particularly poor round at Walton Heath, Valentine Viscount Castlerosse instructed his caddie, "Have the clubs destroyed, and leave the course." Every golfer knows the feeling. As Thomas Boswell observed, "The game of golf was created with humiliation in mind."

Because the game of golf is an exercise in humility, it is wonderful training for life. The thoughtful golfer comes to understand that hazards and bad bounces are simply part of the game. The best thing we can do about our tough breaks is to face them with determined acceptance. And play them where they lie.

You can't get too keyed up about the Bounces a golf ball takes.

● GREG NORMAN ●

Golf is not a game of great shots. It's a game of the most accurate misses.

● Gene Littler ●

Every day on the golf course is about making
little adjustments, taking what you've got
on that day and finding the way to deal with it.

TIGER WOODS

Strengthen yourself with contentment
for it is an impregnable fortress.

EPICTETUS

Little minds have little worries.
Big minds have no room for worries.

RALPH WALDO EMERSON

Accept your disappointments and triumphs
equally.

HARVEY PENICK

Good times, bad times.
They're both hard to grasp.

ROGER MALTBIE

If I could only learn to react differently
between the green and the next tee box
after I have a bad hole.

JIM THORPE

Some players never learn to accept misfortune.
You have to remember that you're not
God's only child of misfortune.

JOE INMAN

A pessimist is one who makes difficulties of his
opportunities. An optimist is one who makes
opportunities of his difficulties.

HARRY TRUMAN

Like life, golf is a game of good breaks
and bad breaks.
There is nothing fair about it.

HARVEY PENICK

Golf is not a fair game and was never
meant to be.

JACK NICKLAUS

Momentum swirls. Golf is not a fair game.
It's a rude game.

FUZZY ZOELLER

There is only one way to happiness and
that is to cease worrying about things
which are beyond the power of our will.

EPICTETUS

WE MUST ALL PLAY THE BALL AS WE FIND IT.

● BOBBY JONES ●

GOLF SPELLED BACKWARDS IS FLOG.

● GLEN WAGGONER ●

Golf is a game of mistakes.

SAM SNEAD

Self-pity is our worst enemy and if we yield
to it, we can never do anything wise
in the world.

HELEN KELLER

Self-pity is the great masochistic tranquilizer.

JACKIE GLEASON

Accept the consequences.
The ball is either going to drop or it isn't.

FRED COUPLES

You can't hate yourself for finishing second.

FUZZY ZOELLER

Golf acts as a corrective against sinful pride.
If Cleopatra had been ousted in the first round
of the Ladies' Singles, we should have heard
a lot less of her proud imperiousness.

P. G. WODEHOUSE

Golf is the hardest game in the world.
There's no way you can ever get it.
Just when you think you do, the game jumps up
and puts you in your place.

BEN CRENSHAW

No matter how poorly you play, there is always
someone you can beat. No matter how well
you play, there is always someone
who can beat you.

HARVEY PENICK

I'm learning to take the bad days better.
This isn't a matter of life and death.

DOTTIE MOCHRIE

Walter Hagen would play a succession of holes
as though divinely inspired.
Then from a clear sky would come a stroke of
unbelievable inaccuracy—a wild slice,
or a top, or a quick, semi-circular hook—and
the heart of the duffer warmed to the god that
could descend to the level of man.

HENRY LONGHURST

Only a mediocre person is always at his best.

SOMERSET MAUGHAM

There comes a time when you realize
you can't fly it over every fairway bunker.

JACK NICKLAUS

Once a time is past, it's past. I have to look to
the future. I have to see what skills I have now.
I can't look backwards, because that man
doesn't exist anymore.

JACK NICKLAUS

Fear not for the future, weep not for the past.

PERCY BYSSHE SHELLEY

Golf brings out your assets and liabilities
as a person.

HALE IRWIN

Don't try to overhaul your basic personality
in order to play better golf.
It won't work.

SAM SNEAD

To play competitive golf you must be
determined, yet resigned.

THOMAS BOSWELL

THE DISCRETION OF A MAN MAKES HIM SLOW TO ANGER, AND HIS GLORY IS TO OVERLOOK A TRANSGRESSION.

● PROVERBS 19:11 NKJV ●

LESSON 10:
APPRECIATION

Enjoy the Round

A happy heart is like a continual feast.
PROVERBS 15:15 NCV

Link St. Clair wrote, "The essence of golf is more than a game; it's a philosophy of life." One of golf's most endearing philosophers was the inimitable Walter Hagen. Hagen instructed his playing partners to "stop and smell the roses." We would all do well to follow that advice. Golf, after all, is still a game. If we fail to enjoy it, we have no one to blame but ourselves.

The next time you tee it up, take a long moment to consider your good fortune. Smell the freshly cut grass. Look carefully at the beautiful scenery. Enjoy the moment. Because in golf, as in life, no one smells the roses for you.

Golf, like life, should be enjoyable.

JOHN DALY

Do you play to enjoy golf or do you
enjoy yourself while you play golf?

CHUCK HOGAN

Golf courses are the answer to the world's
problems. When I get out on that green carpet
called a fairway and manage to poke the ball
right down the middle, my surroundings look
like a touch of heaven on earth.

JIMMY DEMARET

PLAYING GOLF IS A PRIVILEGE, NOT A SENTENCE.

● HARVEY PENICK ●

TAKE PLEASURE NOT IN THE SCORE, BUT IN THE GAME.

● BOBBY JONES ●

Things can always be better, but
they can also be worse.
Why not look on the good side?

FUZZY ZOELLER

I believe playing golf can bring you happiness.

HARVEY PENICK

The clearest sign of wisdom is continued
cheerfulness.

MICHEL DE MONTAIGNE

Always keep it fun. If you don't have fun,
you'll never grow as a person or a player.

TIGER WOODS

Golf is the only game in which one can perform
on the very battleground on which the mighty
have made history. The humble can stand
exactly where the great man stood.
No one, broadly speaking, can play tennis
at Wimbledon or Forest Hills.
Anyone can play at St. Andrews tomorrow.

HENRY LONGHURST

On the golf course, a man may be the dogged
victim of inexorable fate, be struck down by
an appalling stroke of tragedy, become the hero
of unbelievable melodrama, or the clown in
a side-splitting comedy—any of these within
a few hours, and all without having to bury
a corpse or repair a tangled personality.

BOBBY JONES

I LOVE GOLF, BUT GOLF IS NO LONGER AT THE TOP OF MY PRIORITY LIST. GOLF IS NO LONGER MY GOD.

● PAUL AZINGER ●

IF THE SUN IS UP, WHY AREN'T YOU PLAYING GOLF?

● LEE TREVINO ●

Golf is going to test you, but the test is a game.
TOM WATSON

It's not your life; it's not your wife;
it's only a game.
LLOYD MANGRUM

A round of golf should permit eighteen
inspirations.
A. W. TILLINGHAST

Little good comes from brooding about
mistakes. The next shot, in golf or in life,
is the big one.
GRANTLAND RICE

EACH DAY PROVIDES ITS OWN GIFTS.

● MARTIAL ●

THE FACILITY FOR
KEEPING ONESELF
RELAXED
AT ALL TIMES ADDS
A GREAT DEAL TO
THE PLEASURE
OF LIVING.

BOBBY LOCKE

WHOEVER LISTENS TO WHAT IS TAUGHT WILL SUCCEED, AND WHOEVER TRUSTS THE LORD WILL BE HAPPY.

PROVERBS 16:20 NCV

THOUGHTS & REFLECTIONS

_____

_____

_____

_____

_____

_____

_____

_____

_____

_____

_____

_____

_____

_____

THOUGHTS & REFLECTIONS

_____

_____

_____

_____

_____

_____

_____

_____

_____

_____

_____

_____

_____

_____

_____

THOUGHTS & REFLECTIONS

_____

_____

_____

_____

_____

_____

_____

_____

_____

_____

_____

_____

_____

_____

_____

THOUGHTS & REFLECTIONS

THOUGHTS & REFLECTIONS

THOUGHTS & REFLECTIONS

THOUGHTS & REFLECTIONS

_____

_____

_____

_____

_____

_____

_____

_____

_____

_____

_____

_____

_____

_____

_____

THOUGHTS & REFLECTIONS

_____

_____

_____

_____

_____

_____

_____

_____

_____

_____

_____

_____

_____

_____

THOUGHTS & REFLECTIONS

_____

_____

_____

_____

_____

_____

_____

_____

_____

_____

_____

_____

_____

_____

_____

THOUGHTS & REFLECTIONS

_____

_____

_____

_____

_____

_____

_____

_____

_____

_____

_____

_____

_____

_____

THOUGHTS & REFLECTIONS